The Big Red Bus

Written by Alison Hawes

Illustrated by Woody Fox

Collins

A big red bus is at the bus stop.

2

It is the bus to Nut Hill.

We get on the bus.

We get a trip to Nut Hill.

We sit at the back of the bus.

The bus is fast.

We grab on to the rail.

We pass the pond and the clock.

We get to Nut Hill at last.

I press the bell to get off.

Granddad is at the bus stop.

I run up and hug him.

A map

clock

bus stop

pond

bus

14

Nut Hill

Ideas for reading

Learning objectives: Hear, identify, segment and blend phonemes in words; Read on sight high frequency words and other familiar words; Decipher new words, and confirm or check meaning.

Curriculum links: Knowledge and understanding of the world: A sense of place.

Focus phonemes: b (big, bus, back, bell), g (get, grab, granddad), t (at, it, Nut, sit)

Other new phonemes: s, a, i, p, n, c/k, e, o, r, d, u, l

Fast words: the, big, a, is, to, we, of, I

Word count: 79

Getting started

- Write the words that feature the focus phonemes *b, g* and *t* on a small whiteboard and ask the group to fast-read them.

- Choose three or four fast words from the section above, e.g. *we, the, of, I*. Ask the children to fast-read these words in preparation for encountering them in the book.

- Look at the words in the book that include consonant clusters (*stop, trip, fast, grab, pond, clock* and *last*) on the small whiteboard. Model how to blend the *s* and *t* together in *stop* and ask children to attempt to blend the other words.

Reading and responding

- Hand out a copy of the book to each child and ask them to read it independently.

- Listen to each child as they read. Encourage the children to decipher difficult new words such as *grab* and *trip*. Check that they understand the meanings.

- Invite fast-finishers to find out how many times the word *bus* appears in the book. Point out that although it sometimes appears with a capital *B*(in the heading) and at other times in lower case, the word still says the same thing.

- As you move round, check that children understand some of the more complex phrases, e.g. *grab on to the rail*.